JACK AND THE BEANSTALK

by NICK CORNALL

Arranged and edited by ALISON HEDGER

Approximately 40 minutes

The traditional Pantomime story of Jack And The Beanstalk, retold in verse and play, with 6 bright new songs, including some dance, solo singing, percussion and solo descant recorder.

For children 8 to 12 years

MUSICAL CONTENT

INTRODUCTION

#	Song	Performers	Instruments
1	**JACK**	All	recorder, cymbal.
2	**WE LIKE TAKING MONEY**	Bailiffs & All	drums, cymbal, swanee whistle.
3	**RIGHT TO THE END** Farewell Dance	Jack & All	recorder, optional second vocal part.
4	**THE BIRDS AND BEASTS** Animals' Dance	All & Solo	glocks, percussion.
5	**GIANT'S SONG**	Giant solo	
6	**IT'S GOING TO BE A LOVELY KIND OF CHRISTMAS**	All & Solo Jack	sleigh bells, percussion, recorder.

Music for the opening and closing of each scene is indicated in the score.

The PLAY is to be found in the separate PUPILS' BOOK, GA 10492
ISBN 0 7119 29769. This is complete with the song words and recorder part.

The percussion is best learnt by rote.

THE TAPE OF THE MUSIC, GA 10518 is sung and played by ALISON HEDGER with SIDE 2 without singing for practice and performance use.

© Golden Apple Productions 1992
A division of Chester Music Limited
8/9 Frith Street, London, W1V 5TZ

GA 10484   ISBN 0 7119 29750

CHARACTERS

		Speaking parts	Solo singing
	Narrator(s)	✔	
*	Jack	✔	✔ Nos. 3 and 6
*	Daisy	✔	
	Mother	✔	
	Bailiffs: Grabber and Grovel	✔	✔ No. 2
	Wizard	✔	
	Furry Animal	✔	
*	Other Animals		One Animal ✔ No. 4
	Hen		
	Giant	✔	✔ No. 5
	Policeman	✔	

* Indicates characters who dance

GROUP of singers

MUSICIANS to provide percussion and solo recorder, plus any additional sound effects needed.

SIX SCENES

One:	In front of Jack's house
Two:	Jack and cow on the way to market
Three:	By the beanstalk
Four:	Near the giant's castle
Five:	Jack's garden
Six:	Outside the giant's castle / Jack's garden

PRINCIPAL PROPS

5 Magic beans

Beanstalk — an extendable flexible arrangement is best, but not imperative.

Large golden egg

Small tent

LIGHTING

As sophisticated as possible. An ability to dim the stage lights would be an advantage.

COSTUMES

As available - the brighter the better.

Nick Cornall wrote **JACK AND THE BEANSTALK** for his own village school pupils of mixed children up to 11 year olds. The whole school took part in the Christmas production. The narration was read by the Headteacher. If you too wish to involve members of staff in the excitement and pleasure of the Christmas production, this work provides the ideal way of doing it. And no lines to learn!! Just reading from the script.

However, every school situation is different and **JACK AND THE BEANSTALK** will be equally successful performed by a single class. The pantomime covers a spread of abilities and talents. The numbers in the cast are flexible, and can be expanded or reduced as necessary.

For the original performance the pantomime was staged in the round, with the audience at either end. The two sets were fixed and the characters moved within the round as the story progressed. But a more traditional staging will work well, involving just one set change.

Original stage layout

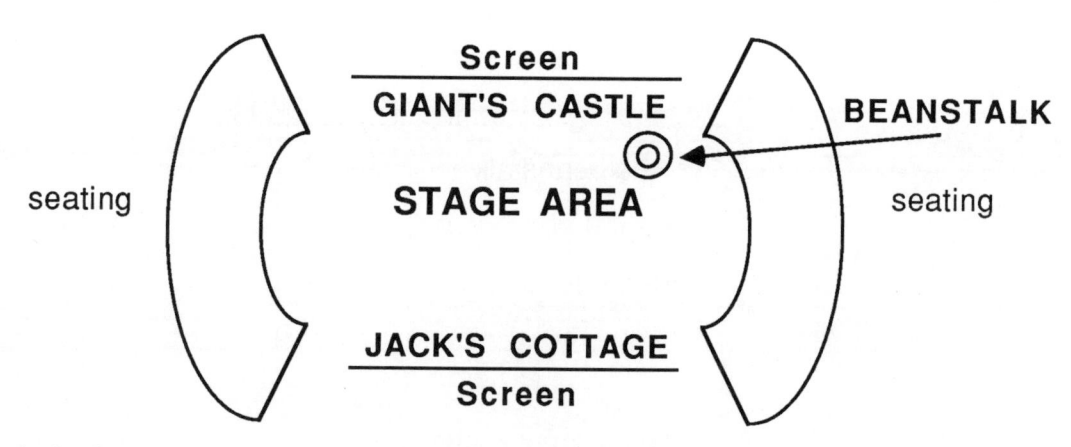

```
                     Screen
                 GIANT'S CASTLE              BEANSTALK
                        ◎
   seating          STAGE AREA                seating

                 JACK'S COTTAGE
                     Screen
```

The technical problem of a giant is solved in the story - he is only three feet 8 inches high!

"Do not worry if your performance is totally unsophisticated - I am sure the fun and sparkle of the play and music will give your school a memorable and happy performance. Have fun!" -

Alison Hedger

INTRODUCTION

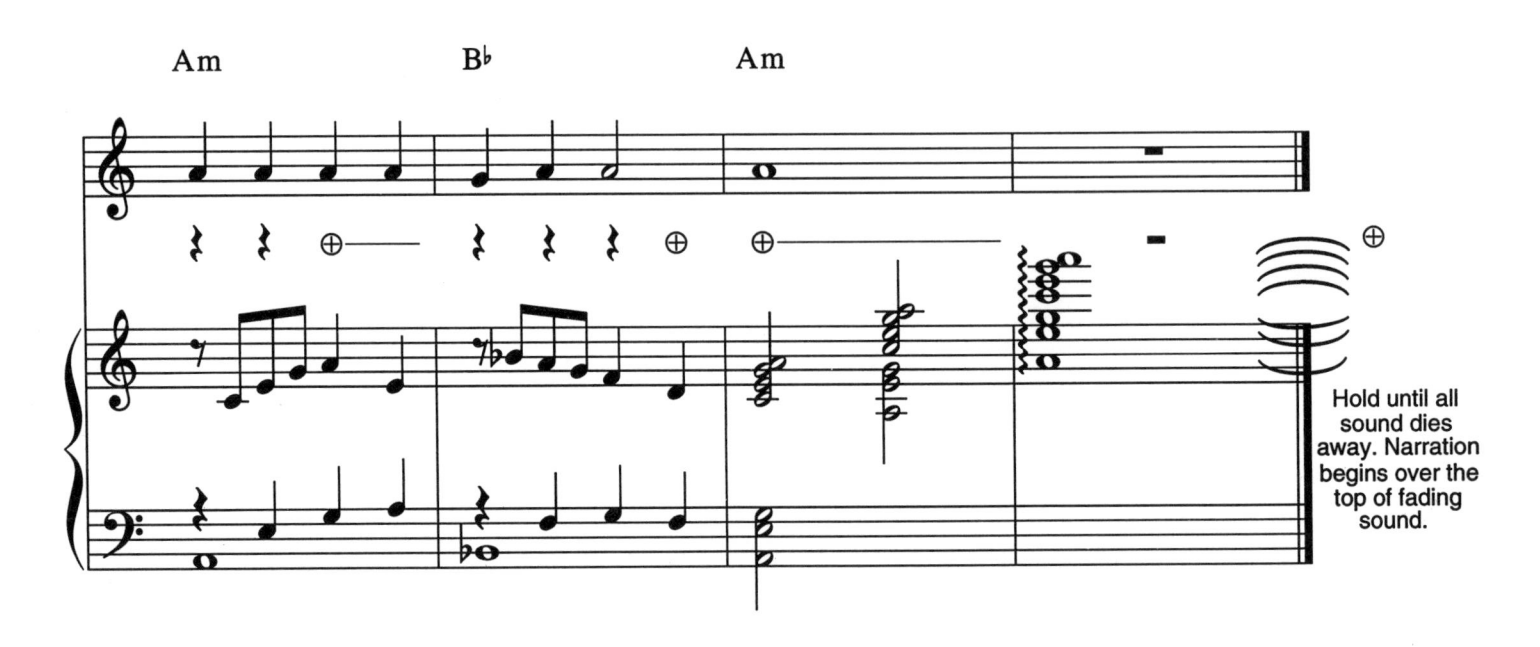

Song 1 - JACK

cue: Well, at least it's fairly short!

Scene three INTRODUCTION: Play VERSE music.   Song 1
Scene three EXIT: Play CHORUS music: (plus singing).

Scene five INTRODUCTION: Play last 13 bars.
Scene five EXIT: Play and repeat as necessary opening 4 bars
                            resolving on an A minor chord.

♩ = 152 Rhythmic and full of life

Am   B♭   Am

This is the sto-ry of a boy named Jack who nev-er had a penn-y
Off to mar-ket one fine day to earn a lit-tle mon-ey the

B♭   Am   B♭

in the bank. All his mon-ey was al-ways spent, he
bills to pay. He tried hard to stretch his means but

never had e-nough to pay the rent. Jack, Jack, his
all that he got was five small beans.

name was Jack. He was nev-er in the black.

Times were hard and times were sad for a cow was all he had.

Jack, Jack, you'll soon be back with the mon-ey that you lack.

You'll find the clouds on high hide a for-tune in the sky.

Jack, Jack, Jack, Jack, Jack. (whispered)

Song 2 - WE LIKE TAKING MONEY

cue: And making them more skinter!!

Scene one EXIT: Play CHORUS music.

Subdivide the two solo parts for the verses, as suits the children taking the parts of Grabber & Grovel.

♩ = 120 Crisp & rhythmic

Cm — GRABBER: Ha, ha, ha, ha, ha.

GROVEL: Ho, ho, ho, ho, ho.

TOGETHER: Hee, hee, hee, hee, hee.

Swanee Whistle

Cm GRABBER and GROVEL:

1. We like taking money and we
2. People call us villains and it's
3. We don't give a present for we'd

G   **Cm**

think it ver - y fun - ny,   es - pecial - ly when they have - n't a - ny
ve - ry true we're will - ing   to e - vict a wid - ow wo - man from her
ra - ther be un - pleas - ant, We like to make the poor feel reall - y

Fm   **D♭**

loot!!   If they're sad and gorm - less and it
farm.   Wait for win - ter weath - er and then
sad.   We are sure that this must be the

Cm   **G**

helps to make them home - less,   Then we think it's reall - y quite a
throw her out what - ev - er,   Know - ing that out - side it's not so
point of hav - ing Christ - mas.   If it is, then Christ - mas ain't so

hoot!!
warm.
bad.
It's so good to be so bad, to lead a life that's mean. Who needs to be good and kind? Be-ing mean's a dream!! Ha, ha, ha, ha ha. ha, HA! HA!

Swanee Whistle

Song 3 - RIGHT TO THE END - Farewell Dance

Song opens scene two - no cue.
Scene two EXIT: Play CHORUS music.

RECORDER FOR v.2 The Farewell Dance - continues through Chorus to Fine.

♩ = 104 Slow tango. Gently and with poignancy

SOLO JACK

1. Right to the end you will be my friend and the sun will
2. *solo recorder*

shine on through._____ I will car - ry on, though my friend, you're gone, but I'll al - ways

RECORDER and OPTIONAL
SECOND VOCAL PART

Through storm-y weath-er, we will still re-

A   D   D   G   G

CHORUS - ALL

think of you. *mf* Through storm-y weath-er, we will still re-

CHORUS

mem - ber. I know I'll nev-er find such a friend as you are.

D   D   A⁷   A⁷   D

mem - ber. I know I'll nev-er find such a friend as you are.

I know for ev - er, we should be to - geth - er. I know I'll

D　　　　　G　　　G　　　　D　　　D

nev - er find such a friend as you are.

A⁷　　　A⁷　　　　D

Last time bar
FINE

pp

Song 4 - THE BIRDS AND BEASTS - Animals' Dance

Scene four INTRODUCTION: Play opening bar several times perhaps varying the octave to retain interest.
cue: He legged it like the clappers
Scene four EXIT: Play VERSE ONE music.
Scene six INTRODUCTION: Play VERSE ONE music.

Glock. notes: C' D'

♩ = 132 Full of bounce

1. The birds and beasts and all the an-i-mals ran a-way, on that day. Ran as fast as feet would car-ry them from the gi-ant's roar.
2. Some folk said that he was terr-i-ble big red beard, slight-ly weird. So they moved their homes and fa-mi-lies from the gi-ant's roar.

3. He was sad and

FINE

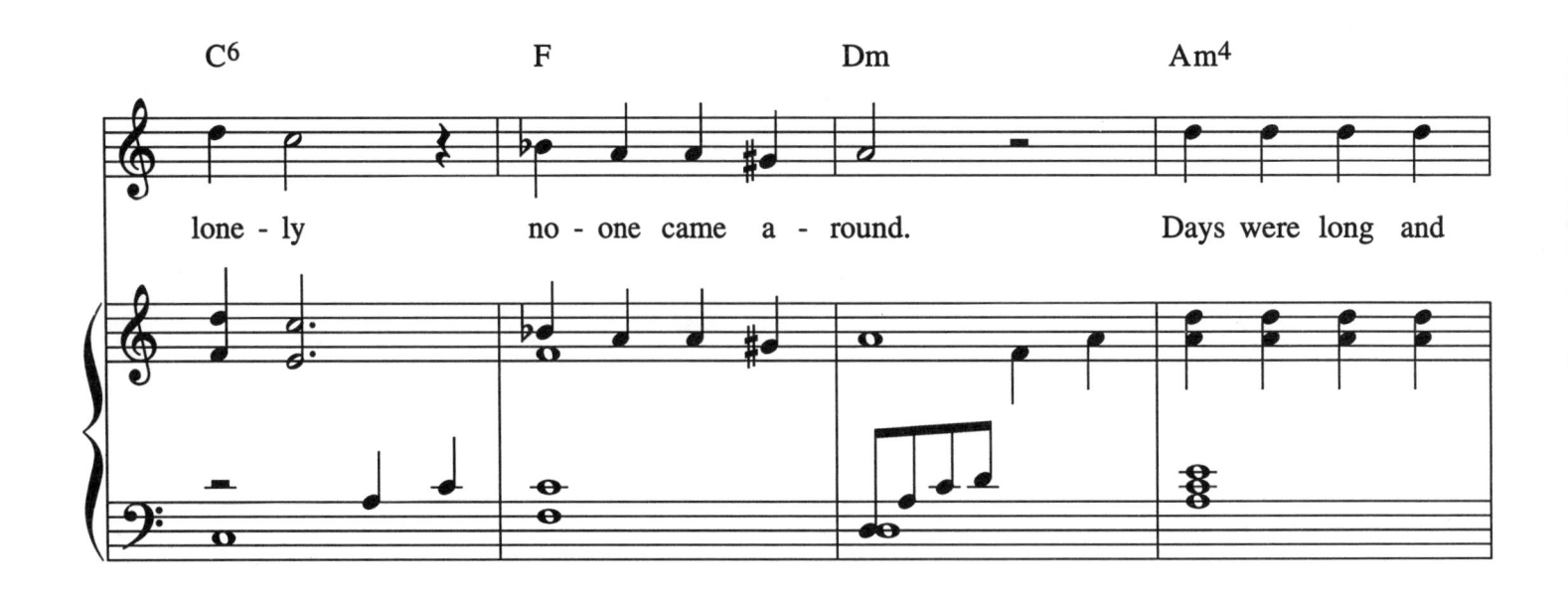

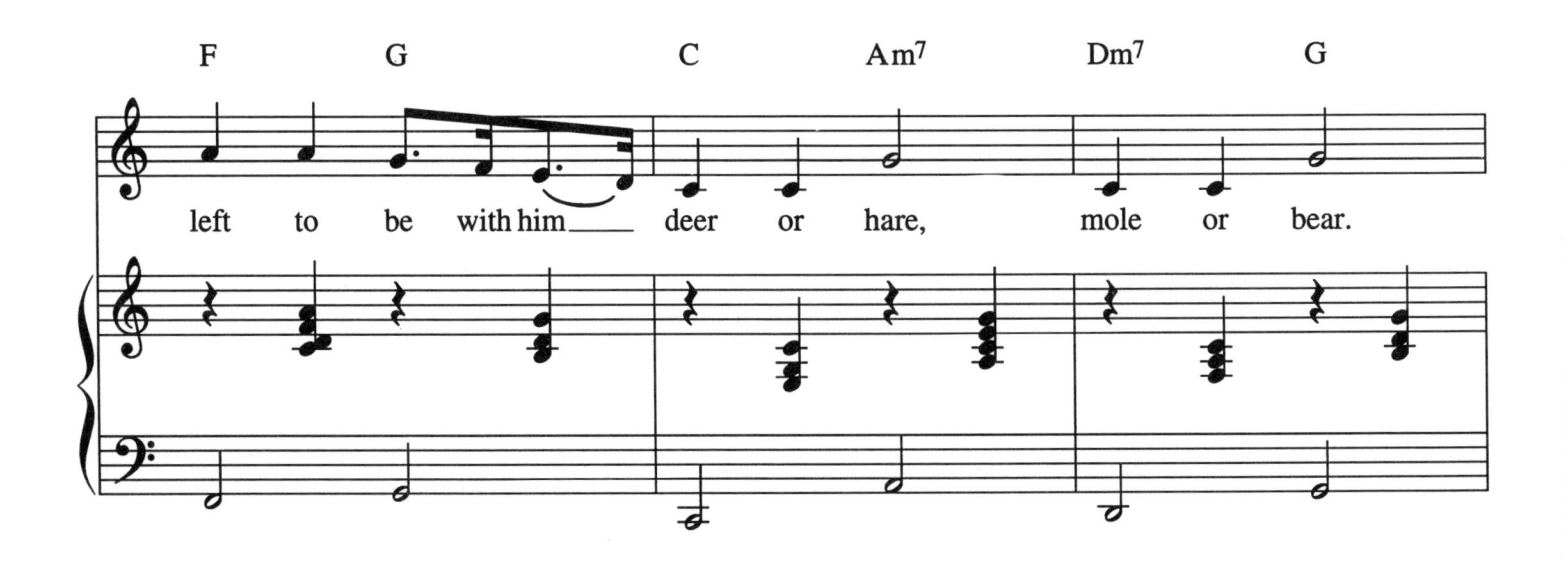

lone-ly no-one came a-round. Days were long and end-less. No friends to be found. 4. Now there's no-one left to be with him___ deer or hare, mole or bear.

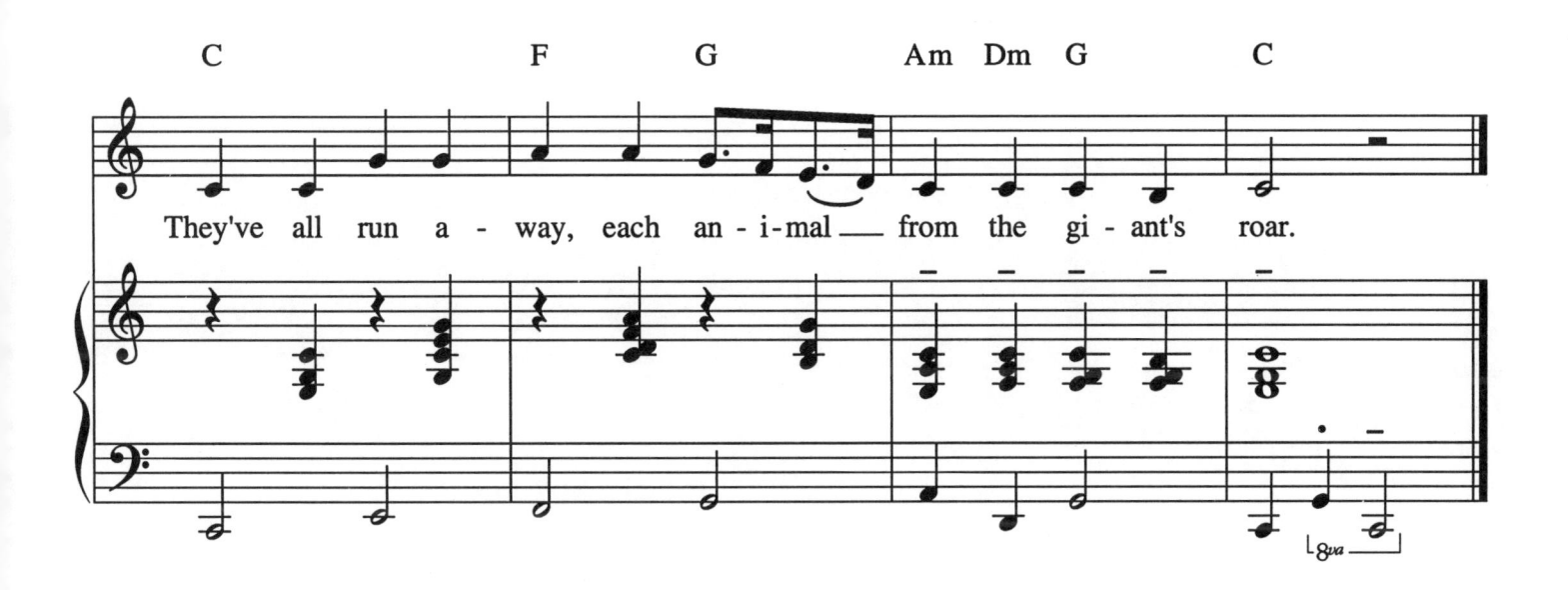

They've all run a-way, each an-i-mal from the gi-ant's roar.

After verse 4 repeat music from verse one, with added glocks and percussion for THE ANIMALS' DANCE - then straight into a sung repeat of verse one (keeping the glocks and percussion) to conclude the song.

GLOCKENSPIELS for ANIMALS' DANCE and sung repeat of verse one.

play 3 times

Use any available percussion for the ANIMALS' DANCE and repeat of verse one. eg. Maracas, tambourines, claves.....

It is best to let the players improvise.

Song 5 - GIANT'S SONG

cue: I HATE being a giant!!

♩ = 152   With steady rhythm & very clear diction

SOLO GIANT

1. I am not a hea-vy-weight. In fact I'm on-ly three feet eight. But here and now I'd like to state I'm not to blame.
2. You try doing the job I do when the min-i-mum height is nine feet two. Des-pite the ex-er-cise I do, I'm not to blame.

| Bm | Em | Am | D |

I know that I'm ve-ry small, not ve-ry tall at all.
Though it's in-ches that I lack, I don't des-erve the sack!

| Gm | C7 | F | D7 |

Oth-er gi-ants may be big. What's tra-di-tion? I've got am-bi-tion!
I know I try ve-ry hard. Be-ing ghas-tly, I'm short but nas-ty!!

| G | | D7 | |

'Cause I'm short don't cri-ti-cise, It's hard-er than you re-a-lise. So
So I try to be quite cruel. It's ve-ry hard. And as a rule I

one more word I'll chase you guys. I'm NOT TO
end up look-ing quite a fool. I'm

BLAME! NOT TO BLAME.

I'm NOT TO BLAME!!

FINE

Song 6 - A LOVELY KIND OF CHRISTMAS

cue: Say "hello!" - It might be Daisy!!

For FINALE play music for taking of bows and exits.

♩ = 184 Full of happiness and good cheer

1. It's going to be a lovely kind of Christmas_____ It's going to be a simply super day.
2. It's going to be a lovely kind of Christmas_____ It's going to be a simply super day.

As dinner plates go

SOLO JACK: When you and I and

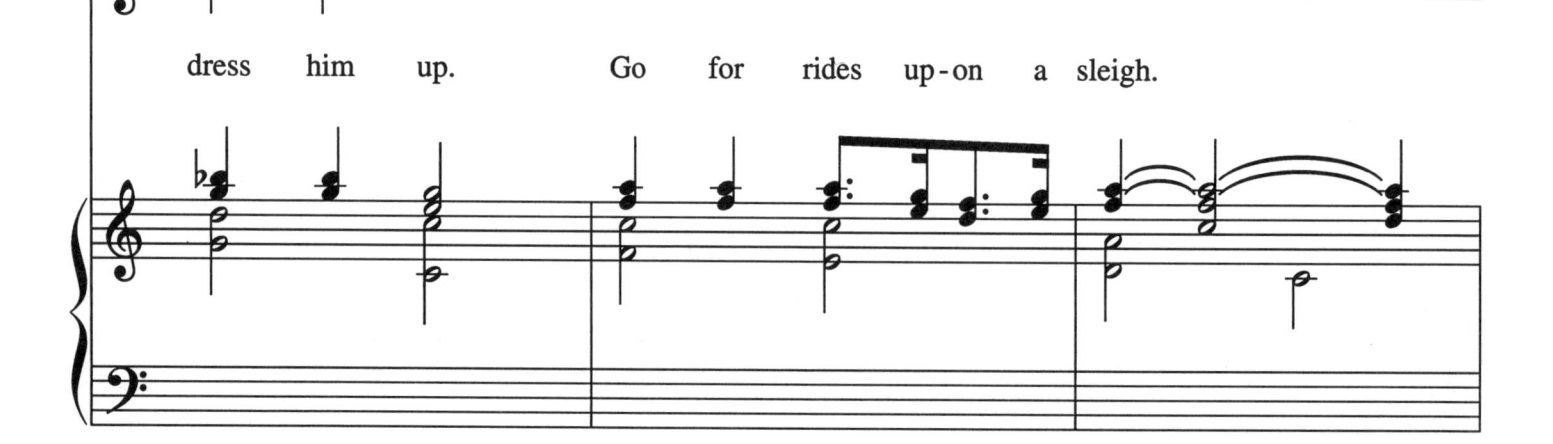

clatt - er, we'll know we're gett - ing fatt - er! Our trou - bles will
Moth - er sing car - ols to each oth - er our trou - bles will

fade a - way.
fade a - way. 3. We'll build a snow - man,

dress him up. Go for rides up - on a sleigh.

O - pen pre - sents round the tree, sing our cares a - way. 4. It's going to be a love - ly kind of Christ - mas It's going to be a sim - ply sup - er day. To car - ols we'll be listen - ing while snow out - side is glisten - ing. Our trou - bles will fade a - way_____ Our trou - bles will fade a - way.

Additional percussion, e.g. maracas etc. are added as desired.
It is best to improvise these parts.